This Book Belongs To.

NAME

"Midnight, Me, & Bob Macabre"

© 2013 Crash LaResh
Illustrations © Tricia Martin
(images pp. 32 & 33 © Gordon Martin)

ISBN10: 1514126982
ISBN13: 978-1514126981

"Midnight, Me, & Bob Macabre"

A Nighty-Nite tale of torture and torment by Crash LaResh
(To be read in an icky Boris Karloff voice)

For Jackson & Gracie Bell

These be the tales of a lad we'll call Vex,
Who was chilled to his bones by a horrible hex.
His problem was rare, but far from unique—
Night after night, the boy never sleeped.
It's clearly agreed that the ripe age of nine
Is surely quite early for losing one's mind—
But never the less, he was coming unglued.
Nothing, and no one, could lighten his mood.

His nightly encounters with things so horrific
Had taken a bone twitching toll most prolific—
To the point where his days were filled with the dread
That nighty nite was coming, almost time for bed.
Inside his head raged a whirlwind so wild—
The monstrous creations of an above average child.
They were running amuck, so out of control—
He'd seen eyes staring back from his cereal bowl!

Maybe his view was a little bit bent,
But that's all that he knew, and so on the day went.
"Get up and get dressed!" screeched the loud wrath of Mum,
In a voice with more turbulence than a nuclear bomb.
"You had better have finished your homework last night,
And clean up that mess! It's a hideous sight!
I don't have the time, so you must get it done!
Get your sister to help you, now I've gotta run."

Sitting up in bed, Vex's eyes scanned the room,
With a familiar sense of impending doom.
"Well, it's not quite as spooky as the night before,
But who knows what lurks beyond my bedroom door?"
Just then, down the hall, came a sound so disturbing—
So cold, so strong, so maniacally un-nerving.
Its power so great that as it grew closer,
The corridor becoming ever so much moroser.

The wooden floor creaked and the walls became twisted—
Vex pulled up the covers as his panic persisted.
The window panes rattled as he shook to his core.
And just as his heart couldn't take anymore,
The door blasted open with a menacing velocity,
And in stormed the Demon of tra-la-la-la-locity.
A three-and-a-half foot tall bundle so cute—
So sweet she could make even Santa Claus puke.

Greeted each morning by this his lil' sister Twink,
She'd skip round him in circles, and give him a wink.
Her hair tied in braids that she'd weaved herself—
Of colored yarn and ribbons like a demented elf.
With her as always, clamped tight in her talons,
Was an evil-eyed ragdoll that looked slightly unbalanced.
It was dressed just like Twink- what a devilish pair,
With their frightful three-eyed, hyper-active hypno-stare.

He pushed her aside with his hand on her head,
Crawled on all fours to the edge of the bed,
Got dressed in his clothes that hung on the chair—
Thus began yet another day fueled with despair.

Escorted by pointy-headed shadows with claws—
Harassed and tormented by their jeers and guffaws,
He skulked thru' the school yard paranoid and deluded,
As malign classroom chitchat left him quite ill-reputed.

"There goes weird kid!"— "Hey freak, what's yer deal?"
The girls that sat near him would point and they'd squeal.
Stiff in his desk, trying hard to stay focused—
Never knowing what's real from what's hocus pocus.
His face was tensed up in zombified trance,
While the words on the chalkboard undulated and danced—
Spinning and twisting, and what happened next?
His bone-wearied head crashed down on his desk.

When forehead met Masonite, it resounded with a THWACK!
Foul wind chilled the air as the creature teacher looked back.
Throbbing with rage, she launched an attack
Of grotesque squid-like arms, reaching out, with a crack.
In one slimy grope, by his hood he was snatched,
And hung in the air like the mornings fresh catch.
The beast looked him over in total disgust,
'Til her internal rage cooker finally went bust.

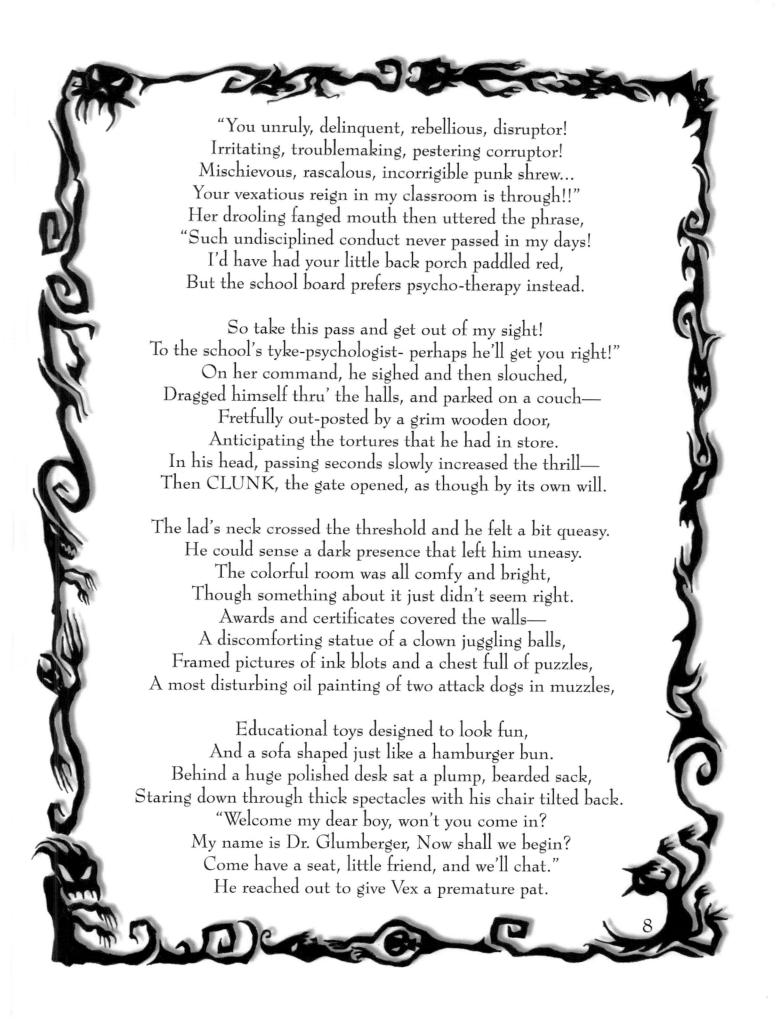

"You unruly, delinquent, rebellious, disruptor!
Irritating, troublemaking, pestering corruptor!
Mischievous, rascalous, incorrigible punk shrew...
Your vexatious reign in my classroom is through!!"
Her drooling fanged mouth then uttered the phrase,
"Such undisciplined conduct never passed in my days!
I'd have had your little back porch paddled red,
But the school board prefers psycho-therapy instead.

So take this pass and get out of my sight!
To the school's tyke-psychologist- perhaps he'll get you right!"
On her command, he sighed and then slouched,
Dragged himself thru' the halls, and parked on a couch—
Fretfully out-posted by a grim wooden door,
Anticipating the tortures that he had in store.
In his head, passing seconds slowly increased the thrill—
Then CLUNK, the gate opened, as though by its own will.

The lad's neck crossed the threshold and he felt a bit queasy.
He could sense a dark presence that left him uneasy.
The colorful room was all comfy and bright,
Though something about it just didn't seem right.
Awards and certificates covered the walls—
A discomforting statue of a clown juggling balls,
Framed pictures of ink blots and a chest full of puzzles,
A most disturbing oil painting of two attack dogs in muzzles,

Educational toys designed to look fun,
And a sofa shaped just like a hamburger bun.
Behind a huge polished desk sat a plump, bearded sack,
Staring down through thick spectacles with his chair tilted back.
"Welcome my dear boy, won't you come in?
My name is Dr. Glumberger, Now shall we begin?
Come have a seat, little friend, and we'll chat."
He reached out to give Vex a premature pat.

His repellent old hand, had a moth-ball-ish odor—
Vex backed onto the sofa and slid all the way over.
The Doctor stood up and cleared his throat with a cough,
As Vex started to speak, the big chub cut him off.
"I've had a long talk with your mother and teacher,
Some esteemed colleagues, your principal, and preacher.
It's been decided, that you're quite in need of my care—
All this odd-ball behavior has stirred quite a scare."

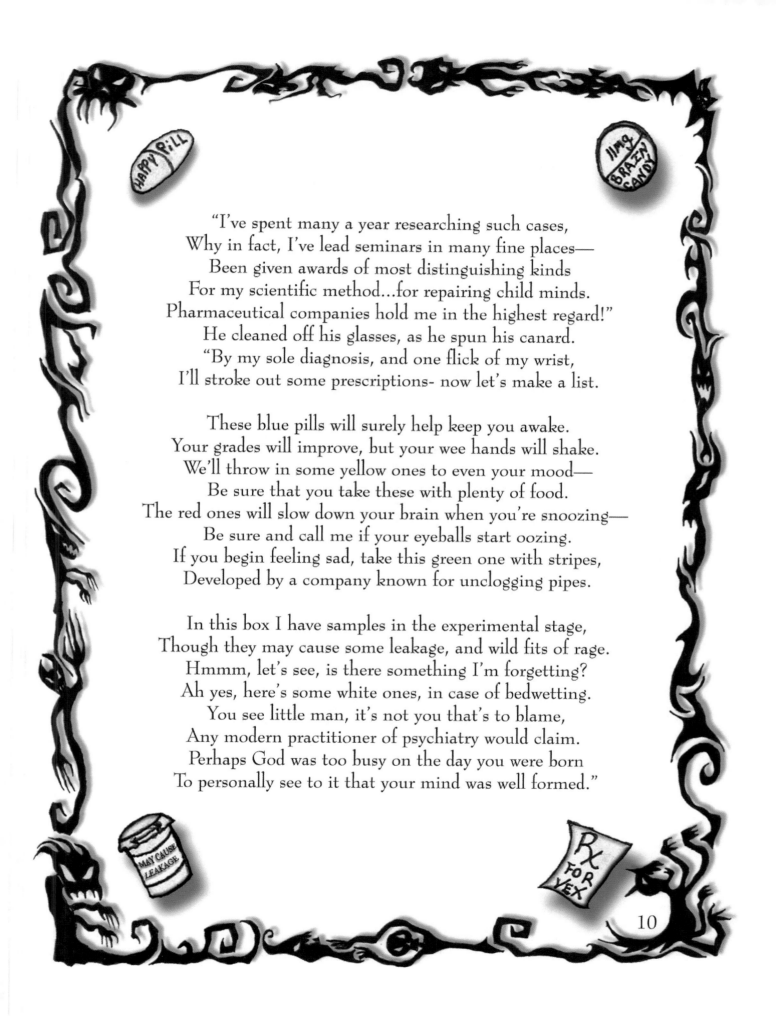

"I've spent many a year researching such cases,
Why in fact, I've lead seminars in many fine places—
Been given awards of most distinguishing kinds
For my scientific method...for repairing child minds.
Pharmaceutical companies hold me in the highest regard!"
He cleaned off his glasses, as he spun his canard.
"By my sole diagnosis, and one flick of my wrist,
I'll stroke out some prescriptions- now let's make a list.

These blue pills will surely help keep you awake.
Your grades will improve, but your wee hands will shake.
We'll throw in some yellow ones to even your mood—
Be sure that you take these with plenty of food.
The red ones will slow down your brain when you're snoozing—
Be sure and call me if your eyeballs start oozing.
If you begin feeling sad, take this green one with stripes,
Developed by a company known for unclogging pipes.

In this box I have samples in the experimental stage,
Though they may cause some leakage, and wild fits of rage.
Hmmm, let's see, is there something I'm forgetting?
Ah yes, here's some white ones, in case of bedwetting.
You see little man, it's not you that's to blame,
Any modern practitioner of psychiatry would claim.
Perhaps God was too busy on the day you were born
To personally see to it that your mind was well formed."

10

"And that's where I come in, to take up his slack—
Seeing to it that all missing parts are put back.
Unlike that Piper that led babes to their fate,
Less than half of my patients become wards of the state."
With all of his might the boy again tried to speak,
But his wide gaping mouth barely uttered a squeak.
Frozen in shock he thought, "They think I'M crazy?
Is this it? Am I doomed? Can nobody save me?"

"How 'bout an experiment to put your mind to the test,"
Said the Doc, "Through Hypnosis, I've had great success.
Just close your eyes, and count backwards from ten—
When I snap my fingers you'll awaken again.
While you're cozily sleeping, I'll be exploring your noodle—
The good thoughts, the bad thoughts, the whole kit n'caboodle.
I shall unleash these 'spookies' that plague you at night.
You'll awaken refreshed- free of worry and fright."

Though the outlook seemed grim, Vex pulled up his hood.
"Can't I just go, if I promise to be good?"
The Doc shook his head, and ignored the request,
Then he pulled an old pocket watch out of his vest.
He then spoke in a tone that was ever so soothing—
As the watch started swinging, Vex's eyes started moving.
Lower and lower, to one side, then back—
His weighted lids closed, and all things went black.

12

A few moments then passed, and from inside that room
Came an unearthly, petrifying, Kaboom of Gloom!
A phantasmagorical spook circus galore
Could be heard blaring out through the cracks in the door.
Rattlings and thunderings, fierce growls and screeches—
T'would've caused the most undaunted to soil his breeches.
An untamable creepshow, therein was ensuing—
A ringside seat for the Doc's private viewing.

Safely unaware with his peepers shut tight—
Protected from the raving, unfathomable fright,
Sat the boy with no knowledge of the riotous scrap
Until suddenly awakened by a resounding SNAP!

Roused by the jolt, would you believe what he found?
Glumberger curled up in a ball on the ground.
Shriveled and sniveling, chubby thumb in his gob—
From pompous old windbag, to knee-knocking slob.

Without further adieu, Vex hopped off the couch,
And took a long step 'round the catatonic slouch.
He cringed at the jiggling lump on the floor,
As he cautiously weaseled his way out the door.
His relief was made brief by the dismissal bell blast—
Embittered with knowing another dark day half past.
Drained of all hope, he sat down in the hall
In a melancholy pose with his back to the wall.

Hoodie pulled up, and head tilted down—
Cloaking his increasing internal frown.
The scent of disaster soon filled the air—
In his bones he detected a cold-hearted stare.
With a shy bloodshot eye, he peered up to find
A dark teratoid of the most evil kind.
His bane of existence, twice held back to sixth grade,
Hall monitoring she-monster, a.k.a. Gank McQuade.

The she-hulk leaned in, uni-brow bulging out.
Stiff with fear Vex felt puke rising up toward his mouth.
A slow motion fist was surely heading his way—
Eyes tight and teeth clenched, he started to pray.
"Rise n'shine little crud!" growled the 12 year old hunk,
Whose breath, by the way, reeked of rotting dead skunk.
"As official hall monitor, I'm delivering this note."
Then Gank pulled out a card from inside of her coat.

She crumbled it into a tight crinkled ball—
With a fresh retched up loogie, hung it up on the wall.
Imparting a departing hairy knuckle to his head,
Took her leave with, "The next time I see you...yer dead!"
Vex peeled off the mucus-soaked memo of scum,
Revealing a message from dear absentee Mum.
It was torn from a pad bearing school letterhead—
Scribed in bold print, and here's what it read...

"Dear son, be advised, I'll be home a bit late—
Hurry home after school, and don't hesitate.
I shall meet you there later with your sister in tow.
Have a good day, now I've got to go!"
By those brief words, he took a deep breath—
With a long discharged sigh, thru' the school doors he left.
Cold and alone, he stood on the front stair—
'Neath the darkening sky, in the bleakening air.

Predicting the worst of all his afternoon jaunts,
He trudged forth thru' the gauntlet of invisible haunts.
Outwitting time's haste by slowing his pace,
As wind-swept dead leaves brushed past his face.
His futile attempts to forestall the night
Were dashed by the indomitable sunset in sight.
The night paid no heed to his plot to belay it—
In fact, it did quicken, as he struggled to delay it.

Dark clouds crossed the sky at a rate most perverse,
As a frenzy of crows flew by in reverse.
Rot-crackling trees stood guard up ahead—
A condemned man's last march that ended with bed.
No more could he hold back the pang of dismay
In the icy cold grip of anxiety's foray.
He blasted for home in a spasmodic skedaddle—
Ten blocks in ten minutes across dusk's field of battle.

Thru' the front door he sped and slammed it behind—
Took several deep breaths to quiet his mind.
Sweat-soaked and palpitating, to the deck he collapsed—
A twitch, with teeth grating, while the panic spell lapsed.
No comfort was found in the following sound—
The jingling of keys, and doorknob clicking 'round.
Stepping over his carcass with little concern,
Mum and Twink passed the floor boy with hardly a turn.

Home from her shopping spree, giggly with cheer,
Mum torqued the fried offspring with, "How was school dear?"
Her oblivious query was perceived quite unkind—
Vex grieved on the ground, and replied sickly, "Fine."
With a twisty-twirl pirouette, Twink approached on her toes,
And appraised her enfeebled bro, upside-down nose to nose.
Gazing hard her eyes spun, then she leaned toward his ear,
And quacked out quite cruelly, "Why are you so weird?!"

Bouncing off in her Twinkity pesterful way,
She left Vex to his stupor, keeping madness at bay.
In his sleepless head, brain cell receptors were popping—
Snapping and crackling with no signs of stopping.
Nailed to the floor with his senses a-tingling,
Churned a houseful of sounds and smells intermingling.
Rattling about in his insomnious grey matter,
He tuned into Mum and Twink's late evening clatter.

19

Mum was caught up in her usual duties—
Speed-cooking a dinner of boiled Mackerel Tofuties.
The malodorous fumes that steamed from the pot
Bore a putrid puissance that could petrify snot.
Tinkering near by, Twink and Doll unattended—
Deconstructing some playthings that they frequently mended.
In their "easy bake" lab of child resistant invention,
They toiled with toy tools outside normal convention.

With an old kitchen knife and rusty broke shears,
A concoction of nail polish and old tricycle gears,
She reached out with split cords to an electrical socket—
No parental supervision whatsoever to block it.
"Dinner!" Mum hollered, interrupting Twink's play,
All the while Vex debating to go or to stay.
This place full of madness could hardly compare
To the chaos occurring behind his buggy-eyed glare.

Conspiracy theories stacked his head with much gore
Of scheming, dark beings living under the floor—
Possibly edging their way thru' the boards,
To enslave him below among spookiferus hoards.
Just as clawed clutches could surround the small stiff,
He escaped narrowly in time's nick, nigh a jiff.
A Vex-ish shaped stain was left fading behind
On the rug like a post-murder crime scene outline.

Vex sat himself down in his assigned dinner chair,
And gazed at the gruel pile of this evenings fare.
With a trembling hand he forked at the chow,
And mumbled, "I kinda' don't feel much like eating right now."
"But you've got to eat something," said Mum, "you're so tiny.
If you lose anymore weight, you'll slip thru' your own hiney!"
Twink burped and chuckled at Mum's little joke,
Though the image of this action caused poor Vex to choke.

Mum's rant grew less tasty as she began to explain
About famished unfortunates on the Serengeti Plain.
"Children in poor countries are forced to eat flies,
While some that I've heard of must cannibalize!"
Vex slow-scooped a glob as to not seem ungrateful,
And forced in a spoonful of flavor most hateful.
Violent war began waging in his digestive tract—
Between mouth and belly, over Mum's home-cooked Gack.

"While you were at school," Mum said, "by the way,
I removed a few things from your bedroom today.
All the horrid old comic books, vid-games, and more...
Your collection of doll heroes, strewn cross the floor—
Every book stretching fantastic, imaginative piffle,
And the posters, and pictures of your creative drivel—
Foolish noise making toys that distract little boys
From their studies and chores- what preposterous bores!"

Mum accounted for this siege with this justification:
She'd been guided by a recent, highly rated observation.
On a one hour episode on her fave TV station,
A celebrity panel cured her maternal frustration.
With one fell swoop of tough Mummy love,
Our twitching young hero was given the shove.
Stripped bare, and left dangling from the cliff of esteem—
All is but lost...or so it would seem.

Mum's tourniquet tongue took a new turn or two—
As many a Mum lecture had been known to do.
"Its 'grow-up' time for you little man.
I've had all of this nonsense that I'm going to stand!
There's no time in the Real World for make-believe foolery—
No excuse is accepted for little boy 'boo-hoo-ery'.
All this nasty, neurotic, nighttime-crazed calamity—
It's sure to evolve into adult insanity!

These nightmare-world 'Spookies' are of your own creation—
An exaggerated case of overdosed imagination,
Easily solved by complete elimination.
The time has now come, for dreamland termination!"
Eyes of the right-minded would've then filled with tears,
But this disordered lad's orbs concealed more worthy fears.
The unending witness to subconscious atrocities—
Gnawed raw by night terrors of vivacious velocities.

Twinged to the marrow of his nine year old being,
Shattered hopeful remains had long been sent fleeing.
Oh, impending sleep be far worse than a spanking—
By which, Mum's fury would not be outranking.
Thus, Mum's many cold words lost their way to his ear,
But what she said next was read LOUD AND CLEAR:
"Go get ready for bed NOW- end of discussion!!"
She announced, unaware of the harsh repercussion.

In the boy those few words unchained fierce reaction
That began with a full-bodied muscle contraction.
From head to toe he was taut, tangled, and twitching,
Then his ears began buzzing with a nettlesome ticking.
From the clock on the wall rang a mocking of chimes
That tocked a death sentence for the lad's sleepless crimes.
Throughout the whole house every timepiece joined in—
Their sadistic bells tolling, "Let the Countdown Begin!"

This vociferous chorus blasted its hymn,
"8:20 PM, nighty-nite, Sonny Jim!"
Though their jibing was fierce, Vex would not take the bait—
He slogged to the sink and dropped in his plate.
Vex turned toward Judge Mum and mewled an appeal,
But his plea was rejected with a motherly zeal.
Grounding her stance her expression grew harsh
As she pointed to the staircase and snarled the word, "MARCH!"

Up three dark flights to his "beddy-bye" gallows
To prepare for the last of all "tucking-in" hallows—
As Vex lifted his foot to begin the ascension,
His noddle was throttled with nightmaric retention.
Each scuffed crooked step wise-cracked and creaked—
Deriving much joy from the poor boy's defeat.
This embittered ole stairway had survived countless bouts
Of kickings and screamings, and scrapings and pouts.

Holding fast to the banister his knuckles turned pale—
Vex crept and Vex stepped, as his hands clutched the rails.
Past evidence of struggles marked his dim upward trail,
With deep scratches and fragments of small fingernails.
Halfway to the top came a trembling sensation.
From beneath his cold feet rose a violent vibration—
Like an oncoming train closing in from behind
Came the Twink loco-motive, tweaked out of her mind.

The Twink loved her bedtime like a piglet loves swill—
Snuggly ugly tucked tight, with a cold bed sheet chill.
She plowed over Vex in an offensive blitzo—
Nearly derailing the sleep bereaved schizo.
He lifted his head, post "hit n' run" dash,
Just to catch a brief glimpse of a Twink n' Doll flash.
They zipped to the bathroom with a brush, rinse n' spit—
Jammied up in two shakes, and to their bedroom they split.

A Mum shout from below gave a push from behind,
"I'll be up for a bed check, in 10 minutes' time!"
Vex took a look back, and then forged ahead—
A farewell trip to the washroom to get prepped for bed.
He scrubbed his glub face as hot steam filled the room—
Letters dripped down the mirror, squealing out the word "DOOM!!"
The face that stared back through the reflective glass,
Morphed into a fiend with a serpentine laugh.

"You Are Done For!" it groaned with a raving mad chuckle,
"Tonight you'll know horrors that'll make your core buckle!
So adieu frazzled youth, and enjoy your crash dive—
For this may, indeed be, your last night alive!"
The lad's gut then did woozle and his feet they did foozle—
Backing over the door jam, he crashed on his caboozle.
He lay stunned on his back in the dark hall of glum—
Barely lit by one light bulb that flickered and hummed.

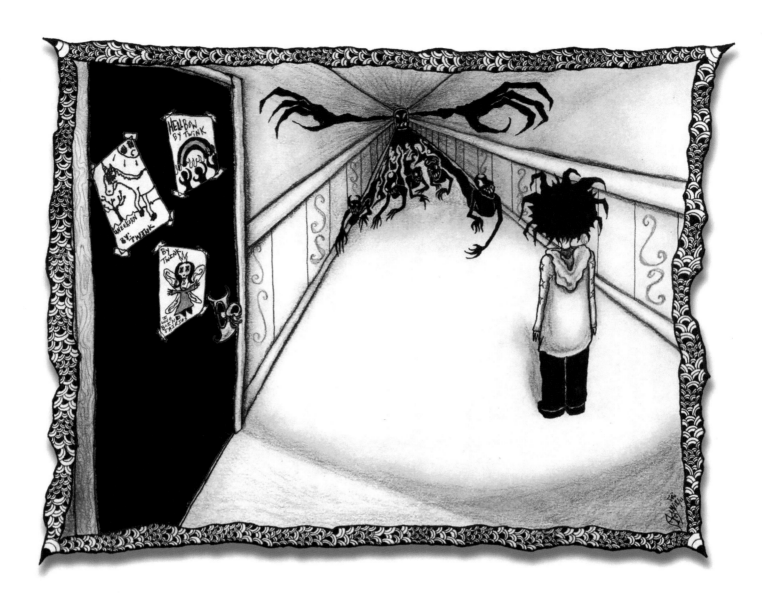

Vex sat up and shook off the spill he had taken,
And lurched down the pathway alone and forsaken.
Up ahead he saw light leaking out 'cross the floor
Through a gap at the bottom of sister Twink's door.
He approached with reluctance this port to Twink's cell—
Painted black, like her soul, with a sweet girly smell.
Covered in unicorns, rainbows, and fairies,
With their eyeballs rubbed out by Twink to look scary.

Inside he spied and heard Mum and Twink's gigglings—
Mum smooching Twink's cheeks, calming pre-slumber wigglings.
Green and lamenting, he turned and proceeded
Down the crookedy hallway, sick and defeated.

The passage dead-ended at a Dungeony door
Which sealed up the doom-room that the sad boy abhorred.
Vex was dwarfed by the wicked Brobdingnagian barrier
That seemed normal by day, but at night twas much scarier.

Huge, with black hinges of wrought casted metals,
And wood that was splintered like sharp cactus nettles—
A keyhole for which no one held the key,
And a rusted ole knob that no one could turn free.
With a trembling hand and red sleepless eyes,
Vex grabbed for the knob, but to his shock n'surprise
The knob grabbed him first by the wrist with a twist,
And squeezed, like a viper, the boy's arm in its fist.

It spun the boy 'round in a full nelson grip—
With one door-slamming swoop, in the room he was flipped.
As Vex flew thru' the air, all his faith was dismissed,
Then he fell to his old bed's "soft-downy" abyss.
Trapped in its quicksandish, nightmarey snare,
He sank deep in its sink-hole of feathered despair.
He struggled to swim to the edge of the quag,
To be barfed from the bed in one bile-belching gag.

He squished on the floor and shook off the delusion,
But the room where he sat was no childish illusion.
The walls had been stripped, tacks and hooks left behind—
All the book shelves were emptied, to de-stimulate his mind.
Just dust, cracks and cobwebs, four walls and eight corners—
The old bed's bent posts stood like pallbearing mourners.
His only escape was one arch-topped stained window,
Separating the world from his dim chambered limbo.

As depressingly heinous as all this may seem,
There was yet one more furnishing that made Vex's soul scream.
More frightening than armies of mummified mimes,
And it casted its shadow on Vex at all times.
Towering nearly eight monstrous feet tall,
And bolted with stainless steel screws to the wall,
Lurked a demonic, ornate, old grandfather clock
That chimed pipe organ dirges by Sebastian Bach.

Chiseled from rotten, old, dark cherry oak,
With a blackened-blood finish that would gag a ghoul's throat.
The top had been carved into two sharpened horns,
And its trunk of a body was covered in thorns.
The face of the beastie was cratered and hanged,
With a jagged cut mouth that was hungry and fanged.
It's time-telling hands were crusty with age,
And each minute scraped by as its clockworks engaged.

Warped planks in the floor cracked under its girth—
At its base grizzly claw-nails dug in with all worth.
Inside its caged torso, a pendulum hung
That klunked and kerrthunked, and chopped as it swung.
The clock drooled, and grunted out, "9:58!"
With a deathly green smirk on its face full of hate.
Vex heedfully hid from the grand tocking thug,
Just as Mum stormed the room with a scowl on her mug.

Her blood pressure soared as her veins began swelling—
A standard operation which proceeded much yelling.
She uncrossed and extended her long Mumly arm—
Unrolling her long, fetid finger of harm.
With a point to the clock, she nagged, "Look at the time!
Why are you awake?! Have you plum lost your mind?!
Get your raggedy bum up, and into that bed!"
Mum yapped as the veins in her finger bulged red.

His wetted red eyes began drooping and dripping,
But Mum butted right in before he could start yipping.
"Yeah, I know," Mum snubbed, "your room's full of harm,"
As she dragged the boy bedward with a pinch to the arm.
"But the closet is dark and quite empty, you see…
No disfigured freak spookie that's trying to break free.
Nothing's creeping outside….the window's locked tight!
Jus' the wind, an old tree, and a shadow in the night."

"There's no pus-covered mutants that hunger for brains!
And no leather clad lunch ladies with hair made of chains!
No green viral ooze seeping in from the ceiling
To burn off your skin while you're writhing and squealing!
Don't fret or concern over reptilian ferns
That strangle small boys with their twists and their turns.
Your room has no big bearded rats with skin rashes—
Nor big headed spookies with snakes for eyelashes!

No conjoined babies with scab covered faces
To bind you and gag you with dirty shoelaces.
Nothing will get you when I dim the lighting,
Now get under those sheets before bed bugs start biting!"
Then Mum put a small kiss in the palm of her hand,
And covered the boy's mouth with loving remand.
"I wish you…as always…the sweetest of dreams,
But try not to wake me with your late night screams."

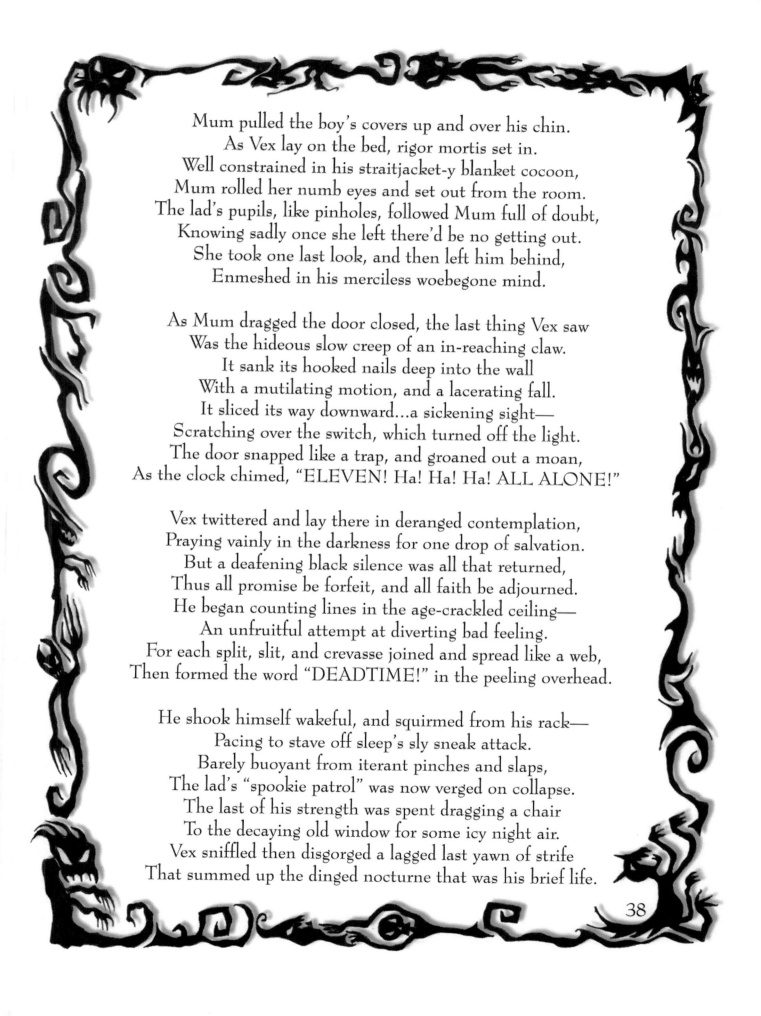

Mum pulled the boy's covers up and over his chin.
As Vex lay on the bed, rigor mortis set in.
Well constrained in his straitjacket-y blanket cocoon,
Mum rolled her numb eyes and set out from the room.
The lad's pupils, like pinholes, followed Mum full of doubt,
Knowing sadly once she left there'd be no getting out.
She took one last look, and then left him behind,
Enmeshed in his merciless woebegone mind.

As Mum dragged the door closed, the last thing Vex saw
Was the hideous slow creep of an in-reaching claw.
It sank its hooked nails deep into the wall
With a mutilating motion, and a lacerating fall.
It sliced its way downward...a sickening sight—
Scratching over the switch, which turned off the light.
The door snapped like a trap, and groaned out a moan,
As the clock chimed, "ELEVEN! Ha! Ha! Ha! ALL ALONE!"

Vex twittered and lay there in deranged contemplation,
Praying vainly in the darkness for one drop of salvation.
But a deafening black silence was all that returned,
Thus all promise be forfeit, and all faith be adjourned.
He began counting lines in the age-crackled ceiling—
An unfruitful attempt at diverting bad feeling.
For each split, slit, and crevasse joined and spread like a web,
Then formed the word "DEADTIME!" in the peeling overhead.

He shook himself wakeful, and squirmed from his rack—
Pacing to stave off sleep's sly sneak attack.
Barely buoyant from iterant pinches and slaps,
The lad's "spookie patrol" was now verged on collapse.
The last of his strength was spent dragging a chair
To the decaying old window for some icy night air.
Vex sniffled then disgorged a lagged last yawn of strife
That summed up the dinged nocturne that was his brief life.

He rolled sallow eyes drenched with weep to the sky,
And held them fast thru' the blackness for the Moon's vigil eye.
For only the mother of all nightness could see
The eclipse in his soul, and thus bare empathy.
Weighted with sorrow the boy's moue nodded downward—
From his high lofty window Vex then caught a glimpse townward.
Seeing hundreds of night-light lit bedrooms go dim—
All babes raptured to slumberland…ALL except him.

Vex wiped a sob glob on his p-jammy sleeve—
Slid off of the chair, and onto his knee.
To the imminent doom he bowed abdication,
But first broke his long silence with this supplication:
"To Whom all nighty-nite things be concerned,
It's me, humble Vex, the paled boy that you've spurned.
For three thousand, three hundred, and ninety-eight nights
I have suffered the worst of your nighty-mare frights."

"For months I've laid in bed awake,
And begged the spookies' grip to break.
For sweeter dreams to be restored—
Such tears I've wept and been ignored.
Beyond my window, I can see
A world of pillowed harmony.
Cozy, Comfy, peaceful faces
Soundly wrapped in sleep's embraces.
Nuzzling off they coo and sigh,
With angels perched on all four sides—
While I toss, and turn and cry,
With haunting shrieks for lullabyes.
Oh, sugared grace of gentle yawns,
Who's cursed the bed I lay upon?
Why 'neath their dozing, calms reside—
But mine, all this has been denied?
Alas, my rival sleep has won—
With reason none, thy will is done.
The bough now breaks, O' Moon, I fall—
Down to The Spookies, Cradle and All."

Never had a bluer prayer ever been released,
And so his conscious drifted off, having said his piece—
But little did our poor Vex know that as he fell dejected,
His woeful call was in fact heard and would not be rejected.
In a coagulation of the falling of moonlight,
Came a gazing of co-miserating from her place up high—
Down thru' the murky, cloud-clotted grey sky.

Swelling up with her tearful lunar heart breaking,
No more could she witness this poor child's forsaking.
Within her cold core came an impassioned shaking—
Escalating quite quickly to a full scale moon-quaking.
Out poured a gush of celestial blubbering,
As she pondered a stop to the child's nightly suffering.
"It seems my spoiled Spookies have been misbehaving—
Running amuck with this boy's nightly hazing.

They must learn their lesson! I must interfere!"
Then she called for the one thing that all Spookies fear.
Not really a thing, but the one special One—
The foe of all Spookies since nightmares begun.
The swaggering depressor of sinful sleep stressors—
The unwrapper of rapscallion foul dream aggressors—
The noxious negator of nefarious nocturnals—
The quixotic opposer of perverse imp infernals.

Who's this that befuddles boogie brutes beneath beds,
And hunts hopped-up hellions from tuckered tots' heads?
Who would dare to go there, in the name of Old Hobb!?
Well…Vex would soon see there's but One for the job.
Back in his dismal dark dungeon of dinge,
Vex was slipping away with his heart cruxed with cringe.
As he lay 'neath the umbra of his old grimly clock,
All the night fell to silence, save for one last "tick-tock".

42

THIS ickety tock-tickety packed a punch, by dog-diggity,
For it ushered the hour known thru' time as sick-sickety—
The wee witching hour that brings magic most sour,
Out of all the clock's digits, big "12" boasts the most power.
Within that split second, the old clock took deep breath,
And filled full of furor its cruel puffed out chest.
It Blanged out it's well known Blarranging Toccata—
A tsunami of sound that could sink an armada.

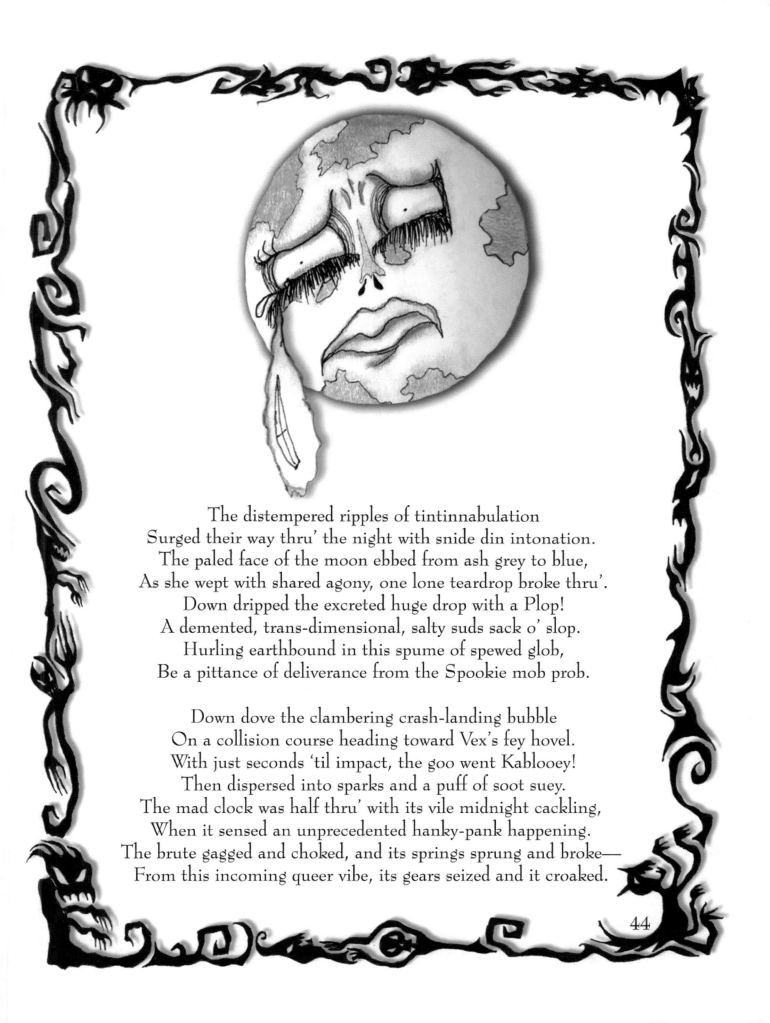

The distempered ripples of tintinnabulation
Surged their way thru' the night with snide din intonation.
The paled face of the moon ebbed from ash grey to blue,
As she wept with shared agony, one lone teardrop broke thru'.
Down dripped the excreted huge drop with a Plop!
A demented, trans-dimensional, salty suds sack o' slop.
Hurling earthbound in this spume of spewed glob,
Be a pittance of deliverance from the Spookie mob prob.

Down dove the clambering crash-landing bubble
On a collision course heading toward Vex's fey hovel.
With just seconds 'til impact, the goo went Kablooey!
Then dispersed into sparks and a puff of soot suey.
The mad clock was half thru' with its vile midnight cackling,
When it sensed an unprecedented hanky-pank happening.
The brute gagged and choked, and its springs sprung and broke—
From this incoming queer vibe, its gears seized and it croaked.

44

The blunt quiet that followed was quickly disturbed
By a room-rumbling ruckus, rousing Vex well perturbed.
The lad ducked in a corner with his eye lids shut tight,
And squealed to himself, "Forgive me, O'Night!"
The room swelled with a thickening black air of doubt,
As if all known reality was being sucked out!
A whirling swirled maelstrom of much marvelling strange
Typhooned the doomed room with topsy-turvy exchange.

The boards in the floor all popped at their seams—
Permeating the air with a green leaching steam.
Arising mid-deck, formed a craggy volcano
That oozed out foul gasses that were muy es no bueno!
A ghostly eruption ensued and then ceased—
Leaving a purple, foamy-fungal, gloppy green yeast.
This "sludge" seemed to move itself a bit well rehearsed—
Rising up like a snowman that melts in reverse.

Then, just as quick as this storm blasted in—
It was gone without trace...the room silenced again.
Curious though reluctant, Vex slow-opened his eyes
To see all was NOT gone, to his ill surprise.
"Huh-hullo?", Vex stuttered as he prepped for a scare,
And he gazed thru' the haze at the figure left there.
His doubting puffed peepers denied what they were seeing!
Ne'er the less 'fore him stood a most macabre unkempt being.

It was gagging and spitting bits of smoke from its throat,
And brushing the remains of green foam from its coat.
To be sure it was like no known creature of lore,
And resembled no Spookie the boy had seen before—
Like a lanky dark scarecrow who'd been vintagely dressed
In a leathery long frock coat, and a threadbare old vest.
Its drooping bell cuffs were torn and distressed,
And sagged down to his elbows with rakish regress.

He was steadily poised with an odd air of valor,
And his pasty skin glowed with a ghoulescent pallor.
Long dreadful locks sprouted up from his crown
Like black, knotty lightning bolt stalks bowing down.
His eyes were concealed 'hind enormous crude goggles—
An "optic-a-ma-jig" pair made o' rivets and brass toggles.
A wide rawhide strap held them firmly in place,
Though their primitive construction obstructed his face.

Bound 'round his thin neck was a long scarf tinged of bone
That moved itself all about with a mind of its own.
The fibrous appendage, so vital and sprightly,
Tugged its master and gestured toward Vex impolitely.
The "being" flipped his collar with Draculean flair,
And turned to the boy with an eyebrow-raised stare.
He leaned down toward the lad with his goggles extended,
While his scarf reached itself up and wiped off the lenses.

Upon his taut face crept a hair-raising huge grin
That played ear to ear, stretching wide 'cross his chin.
Teary Vex still recoiled- trembled cold full of fright
'Til the "being" opened up and his voice broke the night.
"Well, Well, Well, what is this that we have here?"
He closed in on stiff Vex, and looked deep in one ear.
"Hmm…this is quite a bit worse than I thought.
I've arrived just in time! And I'd say not for naught."

He walked 'round the boy, mulling over each inch,
As he poked and he prodded, he speaked as he pinched.
"These nerves in your brain are all frayed and mutated.
What a terrible mess lack of sleep has created!"
Then he pointed two fingers and gave them two shakes,
And shoved them up Vex's nose for heaven's sake!
He waited two seconds then pulled them back out,
And examined the "dipsticks" with his face all a-pout.

"Oh dear, that's not good," He said quite in the know,
"Your nightmare-combobulator's two-twenty quarts low!"
He paused for a moment, and then scratched his chin.
"It's no wonder those Spookies have you left so chagrined."
Vex thought to himself, "Is this spook off its rocker?"
Then the lad bowed his head, and addressed the tall shocker.
"Please forgive me, strange Spookie, I don't mean to be rude,
But WHAT, or should I say who…who are you?"

48

"Bob Macabre....my poor piggy, and I've come from way far
To share and help bare your way through the bizarre.
I can see from that look on your sweet wigged-out face,
You're unclear why I'm here, so let's cut to the chase.
Each night you've cried out to be healed of your hauntings—
To be saved, so to speak, from these cruel Spookie tauntings.
These recurring harsh horrors that rob you of rest
Must be dealt with at once, and for this....Bob's the best!"

Worn out Vex, a rapt listener, was a cynical skeptic—
In his bones he was certain all attempts would turn septic.
"I beg you kind Bob, let it lie," the boy sighed,
"Although many have tried, in the end all have fried!
These Spookies mean business! If I sleep, I am Dead!
As we speak they are plotting a night full of dread!
Your gutty endeavors would be so in vain,
For I know they'll impose spooky pain on my brain!"

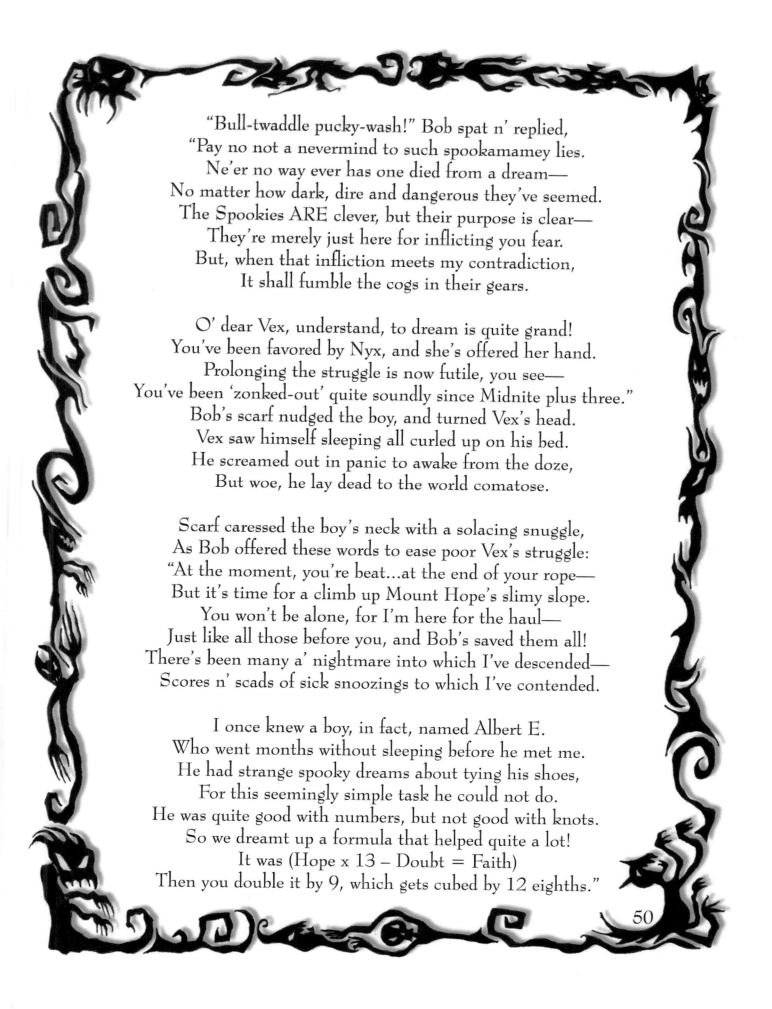

"Bull-twaddle pucky-wash!" Bob spat n' replied,
"Pay no not a nevermind to such spookamamey lies.
Ne'er no way ever has one died from a dream—
No matter how dark, dire and dangerous they've seemed.
The Spookies ARE clever, but their purpose is clear—
They're merely just here for inflicting you fear.
But, when that infliction meets my contradiction,
It shall fumble the cogs in their gears.

O' dear Vex, understand, to dream is quite grand!
You've been favored by Nyx, and she's offered her hand.
Prolonging the struggle is now futile, you see—
You've been 'zonked-out' quite soundly since Midnite plus three."
Bob's scarf nudged the boy, and turned Vex's head.
Vex saw himself sleeping all curled up on his bed.
He screamed out in panic to awake from the doze,
But woe, he lay dead to the world comatose.

Scarf caressed the boy's neck with a solacing snuggle,
As Bob offered these words to ease poor Vex's struggle:
"At the moment, you're beat...at the end of your rope—
But it's time for a climb up Mount Hope's slimy slope.
You won't be alone, for I'm here for the haul—
Just like all those before you, and Bob's saved them all!
There's been many a' nightmare into which I've descended—
Scores n' scads of sick snoozings to which I've contended.

I once knew a boy, in fact, named Albert E.
Who went months without sleeping before he met me.
He had strange spooky dreams about tying his shoes,
For this seemingly simple task he could not do.
He was quite good with numbers, but not good with knots.
So we dreamt up a formula that helped quite a lot!
It was (Hope x 13 – Doubt = Faith)
Then you double it by 9, which gets cubed by 12 eighths."

50

Little Albert called this 'The Certainty Equation',
And it brought him much courage on many occasion.
You see, in his dreams, he learned this simple fact:
Imagination makes Genius, and with that, his fears slacked."
Vex's mind was now jiggly from Bob's rambled prose—
And unable to wake, he begged Bob's interpose.
"Please Sir," the boy pleaded, "You have my surrender."
Then the waif seized the sleeve of his last chance defender.

Choked up by the sad lad's emotive display,
Bob's boo berry eyes fluctuated to grey.
He pulled down his goggles, and flipped back his locks—
Once again cleared his throat, and let out this brief squawk:
"Ahh…Surrender," grinned Bob, "What a perfect beginning!
'Tis indeed most essential If one wants to start winning.
Now tighten your grip boy! It's time to get hopping,
And the best nightmares ALWAYS begin…with a dropping."

With a salient sinking of hoodooed déjà vu,
Vex's tummy grew taught from the Bob's verbal cue.
Something Spooky, he knew, was this way oncoming,
And the foretaste of trauma was grossly tum-numbing.
All at once, in one brisk instantaneous fleet,
The floor began gluggling beneath the boy's feet—
Sludgering into a sawdust-oatmealy goo,
Which our nightmarey duo then glunk-a-dunked thru'.

Swallowed and heaved to a tenebrous void—
A thick vacuum of loneliness where all ease be destroyed.
Pitch blackness unmatched by the sea's deepest places,
Nor the fathomless coves of immersed outer spaces.
Plunging and lowering with no signs of slowering—
A rapid down-diving of declining on-go-ering.
What a chaotic crumbling of tottering stumbling—
This collapsing, descending, non-diminished pit tumbling.

End over end, and sometimes head first,
Vex fell fiercely flailing with his bowels 'bout to burst!
Screaming while G-forces pulled back his face—
Wildly flapping his arms to slow up his pace.
With his eyes tight with fear he repeated this squeal,
"Wake up Vex! It's a Dream! And Dreams are NOT real!"
Then, out of no place, his collar was snagged!
With a shocked sudden stop, his squealing was gagged.

By Bob's clever Scarf the two mates were suspended—
Though Vex was relieved, Bob looked rather offended.
"HOLD IT RIGHT THERE!" Bob concernedly spoke,
"DREAMS BE NOT REAL?! Is this some kind of joke?!
PLEASE pardon my stopping this magnificent dropping…
(And heaven knows how much I love a good flopping…)
But I must explicate for you this instantly,
And emend your snared mind of such vile calumny!"

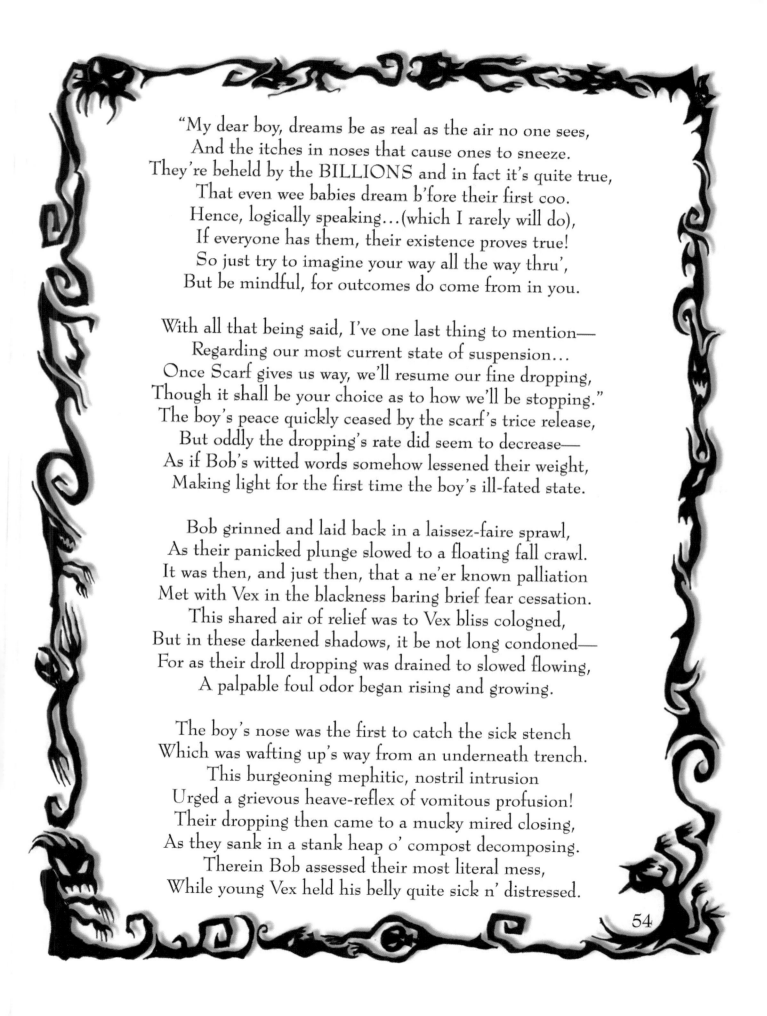

"My dear boy, dreams be as real as the air no one sees,
And the itches in noses that cause ones to sneeze.
They're beheld by the BILLIONS and in fact it's quite true,
That even wee babies dream b'fore their first coo.
Hence, logically speaking…(which I rarely will do),
If everyone has them, their existence proves true!
So just try to imagine your way all the way thru',
But be mindful, for outcomes do come from in you.

With all that being said, I've one last thing to mention—
Regarding our most current state of suspension…
Once Scarf gives us way, we'll resume our fine dropping,
Though it shall be your choice as to how we'll be stopping."
The boy's peace quickly ceased by the scarf's trice release,
But oddly the dropping's rate did seem to decrease—
As if Bob's witted words somehow lessened their weight,
Making light for the first time the boy's ill-fated state.

Bob grinned and laid back in a laissez-faire sprawl,
As their panicked plunge slowed to a floating fall crawl.
It was then, and just then, that a ne'er known palliation
Met with Vex in the blackness baring brief fear cessation.
This shared air of relief was to Vex bliss cologned,
But in these darkened shadows, it be not long condoned—
For as their droll dropping was drained to slowed flowing,
A palpable foul odor began rising and growing.

The boy's nose was the first to catch the sick stench
Which was wafting up's way from an underneath trench.
This burgeoning mephitic, nostril intrusion
Urged a grievous heave-reflex of vomitous profusion!
Their dropping then came to a mucky mired closing,
As they sank in a stank heap o' compost decomposing.
Therein Bob assessed their most literal mess,
While young Vex held his belly quite sick n' distressed.

Bob pulled down his goggles while Vex prepped for demise,
  As a miasmatic fog stung n' scraped at their eyes.
  From atop the heaped pile of stinking bilge waste,
  The two took a look 'round the stygian cessplace.
  "Oh, Bob..." outcried Vex, "I know this dank space!"
His voice quivered with terror as the brume veiled his face.
  Yes, he'd been there before on a previous excursion—
  On one of his many freakish nightmare immersions.

  Bob stood up and took up a stance- arms akimbo,
  And sniffed a bull snort of spook-swamp air, by Jimbo!
  Around the stank heap stood a huge lead balustrade—
  Maligned and aligned, and braced for blockade.
  Bob flipped his lapels- standing tall in command,
  And said, "Stick closely boy, there be mischief at hand."
  To distract the scared lad he engaged this thought swap
  Asking, "What say you, boy? Of this dark bolstered prop?"

"Wwwell," quivered Vex who feared to begin,
"A fence is to either block out….. or lock in.
Either way Sir, this is looking un-good,
And I'd very much like to wake up if I could."
"Wake up? From a Dream?!" blurted Bob, "What a drag!
Why, there's so much more spook-a-dook fun to be had!
We're just beginning this wild nightymare roll!
Great strange things be coming, yes on this, bet your soul!"

As Bob's rant rumbled on, the boy's focus diminished,
And his eyes wandered upward whilst chatty Bob finished.
They widened like portals and welled up with tears,
For what he be beholding filled the child whole with fears.
In benumbed stupefaction he pointed above,
And cut short the Bob who was quite devoid of.
"What is it, Dear boy?! What cat's got your tongue?
You look like a spring in your noggin's un-sprung!"

56

And on that final quote, a huge slobbering glob
Dropped, with a splat, on Bob's dread covered knob.
His eyebrow raised slowly, and an eye shortly followed—
Bob pulled up his goggles, and then anxiously swallowed.
It would seem our two fellows were upon being spied,
As a growing hot growling came down from up high.
Looking up, they were dwarfed by a drool dripping mouth—
Baring gigantic canine teeth that were as big as a house!

From a ginormous, bow-wowing Cerberus beast
Came a barking succession that could rouse the deceased.
The fierce doggie-guard monster snapped, snarled, and groaned—
Nearly blasting the skin off our boy's shaking bones.
Vex took hold Bob's leg and bewailed a shrill cry—
Then the creature lunged forth with red flesh-famished eyes.
A great iron chain clinked, nearly snapping each rung—
Dead halting the vile monstrous doggie fiend's lunge!

Hung high and held back, the beast barked and it spattered—
Its drizzling drooled volumes left the boy's nerves tat-tattered.
It was choked back, just a smidge, from the wee Vex's hull
By a massive dog collar made o' kitty cat skulls.
O' what great dreadful woeing this spooky instilled,
Over many a night spent filling poor Vex with chills.
A brute demon tyrannicus, violent and bullified—
The lad's lifelong uncertainty be therein personified.

Positioning himself between boy and dog,
With his boots planted firm in the squishy rot bog,
Bob knotted up Scarf and struck out a sharp slog—
Whomping the bully pup's snout with a flog.
"Avast!" barked back Bob, "I'll have none o' that!
I am Bob Macabre! Not some skitt-mangy cat!
And your exasperation of this here, my young friend,
Has officially come to its nightly scare end!"

The beast looked at Bob with a long look, unamused.
T'was clear that its pea-sized dog brain was confused.
So, Bob cleared his Bob throat, and issued command
In a dogified speech bully dogs understand,
"GRRRRRUFF!! Gruff Gruff Grrrrrrowl!
GRRAALFF!! Grupp Grupp GRaawwwL!
BrRRaawwwwl Lrrrruff Bruff Braawl?!
Baaaawl? Brrruff Rrruff Grrrrrowl??"

Then the monstrous n' mongrely morbid mutt's head
Moved in toward Bob's ear growling grunts full of dread.
It muttered and mumbled, a closed-mouthy marled message—
The looks of which filled anxious Vex deep with presage.
"Wwwell?" the boy mewed, as he tugged at Bob's coat,
"Are we now to be chawed, chewed n' chugged down its throat?!"
Then Bob leaned with an elbow on the pooch's proboscis,
And smirked as he pet its schnozzola colossus.

"I can see from your twisty boy-face, squinched and straining
That this odd situation is indeed in need of explaining.
You see, this big, blunt, bawling quadruped beast
Claims we've disrupted his nightly dog feast.
It seems we're not standing in a mucky-muck squish,
But in fact, we're knee deeply-deep in his food dish!
So his vicious demeanor's understandably so,
And you're both fairly guilty of each other's caused woe.

Oh…the fright filling horrors we deem mean in dark dreams—
They're so often, quite never, as ill-meant as they're seemed.
Take this spooky for instance, right here, if you would—
Just a misunderstanding 'tween Eater…and Food."
For a moment Vex stood slackly, dropping his jaw.
Then he shook as he spoke with a lump in his craw,
"Please forgive this intrusion, o' big spooky dog creep.
It was not our intention to foul your food heap."

His eyes welled with a fearful tear-filled dilation,
As the boy plead removal from this hairy location.
Then the merciless mutt-mongo's mouth full of might
Came down toward wee Vex with a barbarous brute bite!
But the flesh cleaving crunch that the lad was expecting,
Was halted just one or two chomps from connecting.
In its stead came a fly-papery, slime lick-sticky, tongue
That slung Vex n' Bob in the air with one flung!

Up-over and out of the dish they were thrown—
Discarded like many an ol' mauled up soup bone.
From proverbial "frying pan" now "into the fire",
They were launched by the doggie guard into the mire.
Thus our doomed crew of two through the olid air flew—
Thru' the thickened yuck yonder of nightmare bile blue.
By the viscous sky-stink they were soaked as they soared—
Not the foggiest known notion of what lie in store.

Beaming Bob lead this plight with his goggs strapped just right—
Strangely joyful of this, their fog filth flopping flight.
Good ole Scarf followed suit, stretched out tight, in a twist—
While Vex held fast its end, for dear life, with both fists.
From his nose to his toes, every Vex bone was shivering—
With his face white with fright and tight bloodless lips quivering.
He begged with all might for an end's quick delivering,
Which then it did come with a bum scorching skriddering.

To eventual halt they did bump, skid, and grind—
Leaving torn smoky trails of burned butt bits behind.
Un-tumbled and grumbled, they eyed up to find
A blobbed blimp of a bloke, boiling mad out his mind.
A fierce flob of flab fattitude…an offensive obesity—
Steeped foul with aromas of warm road-killed deceasity.
A bloated beast beef-a-noid monster of mush—
Twelve foot tall, as it's wide, of rolled mucous flesh gush.

And strapped to the back of this cramping fat cuss…
Was a strange, pumping mechanized apparatus.
A slurping and burping Distiller of Drizzle
That filled him quite full with a bubble-ee fizzle.
Chafed raw and enraged, he stood over the pals
With his bulging boiled brow gnarled up into a scowl.
Dripping with sweat, the hobglob groused in a crouch—
Vex's horror was growing, AND so was the grouch!

Inflating with gurgling from its feet to its jowls—
Like 2 tons psi being pumped to its bowels.
The gassy filled devil reached out for the lad,
Belching this introduction with all that it had!
"I am the Fat Hated FLART of Flartoon!!
And I mash Kiddie Souls in my Goon Shaped Spitoon!!
And you, little BOY, smell ripe for the Scrunch!!
I shall boil up your innards for my 'Fizzy Flart' Punch!"

The FLART's halitosis blew primal and heinously
Causing the two to throw up simultaneously.
Closing their nostrils with firmly clamped pinches,
They struggled to fend off its demon stank stenches.
Ducking under Bob's coat, the boy hastened to hide—
But with one fat FLART finger it bumped Bob aside.
By a huge hammy hand Vex was nabbed by the meanie...
And shook upside-down like a nightmare martini.

The slimy FLART's face then grimaced and glistened,
As he oddly held Vex to his ear for a listen.
He was hoping to hear the boy's inner fears fizzin',
For it was fizzy fears that his "Flart Punch" be missin'.
At this point, wee Vex was the world's scaredest boy—
Which of course, brought the FLART the world's mostest joy.
The Flart yucked, "My Flart Punch will now be quite the killer!"
And he whacked and sacked Vex in his back-packed Distiller.

Vex wiggled and willed, and wept in vain struggle—
Nonetheless, fading might dragged him deeper in gluggle.
This poor broken child in tear-weakened defeat,
Reached out his faint heart with this beaten screech-speak...
"Help me, BOB!! No more can I hold on this way!
I am doomed to dissolve here in fizzing decay!
Shall my heart be diluted to quietus beat??
I'll be oozed, brewed, and stewed from my head to my feet!"

One by one the lads fingertips did lose their grip,
And down in the Flart's fizz-machine he did slip.
Scratching and scraping with a cascading sob,
Went the dimming wee Vex his voice crying out..."BOB!!??"
A grotesque gargled gloat laughed up from the Flart's throat—
Spatting spittles of sputum upon Bob's frock coat.
The Flart drooled as he jibed, and he pointed in jest,
As unamused Scarf wiped the spew from Bob's vest.

With one creeping peeved eyebrow peeking over his goggs,
Bob pulled down his specs to appraise the foul hog.
Smiling huge like a child riled and ready for play,
Bob bounced and announced, "Rotty Beastie! Belay!
Forgive me Flartoonian, for exceeding my station,
But your pernicious plot shall soon reach full dilation.
And your Flart-Punch consumption of Fear-Fizz degradation
Is worsening and worsening your gastral inflation!"

"Thus before I'm too late for my friend's liquidation,
I must stymie your pre-victory salivation,
With a gift to YOU Flart, of a squeeze and deflation,
So hold fast for one mamma-jam Flart flatulation!"
All at once eeky Bob, in one half of one tick,
Withdrew cheeky Scarf from his neck slicky quick.
He lassoed the the fat gassy gremlin of bigness,
And cinched up and squinched Scarf around th' Flart's midness.

Punch bladdered, the big bloater blistered and bucked,
With Bob's spook-stomper boots 'gainst its Flart gut o'yuck.
Ole Scarf was stretched tight, to its absolute limit—
While the Flart filled to full from the fizzing fears in it.
Bob squashed the huge lout with all of his clout,
And called to small Vex with this cautioning shout,
"Be brave and be braced, boy! Relinquish all doubt!
For what fills this Flart up is about to come out!"

In the dark name of Nyx, Oh how it did come!
Thru' a fat-folded crack somewhere near the Flart's bum!
An unholy bum-drumrollee blowout supreme
That rip'o-blat-splat-splodey'd thru' Flart's butt seams!
All this breakage of impacted terror-tot blockage
Bursted Flart into pieces from releasage of stoppage.
And the re-volting, rupturing, rot-drenched expulsion
Of pressurized unbridled bung-mung repulsion...

Vaulted Vex from his trap in one gas-gusting heave!
T'was a stank blast of freedom that bore his reprieve.
Such a vile force majeure begot shockwaves and quakings
That rumbled the whole nightmare world with its shakings.
Vex was tossed to be ruined and racked in the blackness,
Surrounded alone by much wreckage of wackness.
He called out to the darkness, "Is anyone there!?"
But his words met damp end in the deadening air.

In this "After-Flart" coated sump cavern of oozage—
In thick puddled yick he sat, rubbing his bruises.
With his hands, heels, n' bum bogged in Fizz n'gut-gloozage,
His eyes gooeyed up with tearglops of confusage.
"Enough! Pleaaase Enough!" Vex shouted his plea,
"Be there no spooky end to this tormentory?!
O' why must I bear my last shortly lived night
In a plague of non-stoppable terrorous frights?"

But all the lad heard in this black undercroft
T'were the drooling stalactites that dripped from aloft.
With sinister "PLOPS" just enough spaced apart,
To bring cruel well-placed shocks to his petrified heart.
Once more Vex deplored, most despondently daunted—
Throwing ricochet echoes of "HELLOoos" most haunted.
Their fade to grim silence was then broken by taunting,
And this peal that returned was one none would be wanting.

Spookish surrounding sounds crunch snapped n' clickened—
Suck-sloppity-plopping, they creeped up and they snickend.
Then out from within the dark shadows emerged…
A most hellish-bent gaggle that were Vex-ly converged.
T'was a gruesome, wee ravenous army of dregs
That were primed for invasion on tentacled legs!
With infesting intention they roached forth for the kill,
As their horrid head honcho announced their cruel will.

The Vermin's Spook Dictator stepped to the front—
Poised firm at attention, then growled with a grunt.
It gripped its foul fist tightly 'round a long staff,
Which it staked in the ground as it snickered and laughed.
This "Nastwatzy Wug" bug king then raised up his hand,
While behind stood his brood, ripe 'n brewed for command.
With his face all galled up, gushing prideful resent,
He conducted the Wug gang's ensembled intent:

"We're rollzee, We're pollzee,
We'll creep in your holesies...
We're Nastwatzy Wug Bugz,
O' so foul and unholy.
We've come, little Nom,
To munch munch you alive...
Writhing in thru' your out-holes,
We'll YUUMPT your insides!!
Now our hungers be great,
And your innards be large...
So rise up, brother Wugzies!
In this Vex let us CHARGE!"

Then the swarming stampede of suck-puckering legs
Wound a Spooky Wugz Wagon train 'round tasty Vex.
With drippy fangs smackling, they approached snackly cackling,
BUT were harshly disrupted by an incoming tackling!!
Off a droppling did dripple from a stalactity nipple—
An oncoming plopple, and an increasing whistle.
It started quite softly, but grew quickly to deafening—
T'was a down stomping BOB with huge BOB boots a steppening!

The look on the angry Wug King turned befuddled
As 9/10ths of his army were turned Wug Bug puddled.
In one Wug splatting splash, ole Bob squashed the bugz feast,
With the Bob Macabre boots on his Bob Macabre feets.
"Well hello, old King Wug! How I've missed ye', me hearty!
And it seems I'm nigh late for a Wugz dinner party.
Why, the whole spookyworld knows Bob loves a soiree—
All th' romping and dancing, and scared-kiddie fillets."

Bob clumsily twirled, squishing more as he sailed—
Th' remaining bowed Wugzies thus speedily bailed
Leaving the bully Wug King left aloned...
"It would seem little King," grinned the Bob, "You're dethroned."
Bob then bid fond farewell to the bully bug schmuck,
As Scarf sent the Wug soaring with one brisk Scarfy pluck.
He turned to wee Vex, whose frayed nerves were now chilled—
Most thankful indeed that his holes were unfilled.

Then something hap't that had not in a while…
Th' bittiest bit semblance of a long lostest smile
Peeked its way through the saddest lad's fear frozen frown—
What had once been misplaced from this face was now found.
Proudly, Bob met this smile with revealing replying,
"I can see you now see…there's no need for a crying.
For there are no Bad Dreams, but some do run awry,
And this fact, little Vex, can't be seen thru' soaked eyes.

So let them be dried by this glorious truth:
The twists in your turns come from twists inside you.
And of all Day's adventures, not a one can compete
With the games you'll now play in the Nights as you sleep.
But before we continue, I shall fix how you're peeping—
Your tear-clouded blinders must see all that is creeping.
So relax, lil' ill piggy, and squeeze those eyes tightly,
And I'll give you a gift to make Spookies more sightly."

Re-fueled and reposed, Vex closed up his eyes—
He took a deep breath, and exhaled a small sigh.
So pleased to see this, Bob grinned side-to-side wide,
And bestowed his great prize on the brave boy with pride.
Scarf flipped back Bob's locks, and slipped off Bob's huge specs.
With a slip, snap n' clasp, Scarf then fit them on Vex.
Bob stooped and leaned close to appraise his fine work,
And he whispered these words thru' his Bob Macabre smirk:

"Somehow, my dear boy, way down in your under...
The dark veil of Fear hath snuffed out all your wonder.
Robbed, as it were, of your childish cognitions—
Left high n' dry with no playful ambitions.
After thirty-three hundred and ninety-eight nights
Of the nastiest nasties of nighty-mare frights,
It's high-time indeed, that this curse be undone...
Now open those eyes boy, and let's have some REAL fun!"

To Be Continued...

A HUGEnormous Thank You of huge enormity to all of our donors who
helped support us in our efforts to bring this book to the sleepless world!

Akiko Toida
Anna Anderson
Anna Russell
Ava Irving
Betsy Mullenix Sheppard
Bobb & Audrey Dymarcik
Bobby & Michelle Scherberger
Daniel & Jennifer Summer
Debra Grant
Denise Brown
Denise Mills
Dennis Bounds
Derick, Ashley, & Dexter Reid
Diana Johnson
Dori Fleischmann
Emma Bass
Emme Greer & Morgan Foster
Erin N. Diaz
Gary Streiner
Gina, Dan, Lenore & Sylvia Dougherty
James & Alex Murd of Crazed Pixel Comics
Jason Avery
John Acheson
John Amplas
John Kirch
John Williams
Junior & Kimberly of One-Eyed Doll
Justin Streiner
Katie Teardrop
Kearston Dillard-Scott
Keith Fogg

Kitty Barnes
Kyra Schon
Ladyhead Heather Free
Lisa Sands
Lisa Shaughnessy
Malaika Albrecht
Marilyn Kellam
Michael Calandra
Mike Cunningham
Nancy Pope
Nikee Harris
Phyllis Pancella
Rachel & Sage Chapin Greenberg
Rachel Scott
Roberta Brennan & Johnathan Adams
Sandy Trapp
Susan Porter
Seth Moody
Shena Ross-Fortson
Steve Shives, Ashley Hutson & Ottie
Steve Czapiewski & Janet Powell
Socko Jones of Comic Book Jones
Sue Eddins
TJ Williams (Gzzzzt!)
Tiffany Fordham
Toni Hollowell
Tegan & Michael Monstor
Thom & Cat Carnell of Zed Presents
Tom "The Lurd" O'Donnell Jr.
Tony & Kerryn Markulin
Witch Hazel

Also, Thank You to all of our anonymous donors & to
everyone who helped spread our campaign around. You are all
most appreciated :)

73

Tricia's Happy Dedication Page

So many people have encouraged my arts & supported my ways of weird over the years- I love you all so very much! I'd like to dedicate my parts of the book to the following amazingly awesome peopley-creatures:

Amanda "Deeda Bug" Haynes. RIP lil' sister. I miss you every day and will never stop loving you!
Also, to her son AJ, sister Jennifer, brother-in-law Dan, and to her mom (and my "Kentucky Mom") Linda. You are all amazing!

My SpouseMonkey Gordon for all his awesome animation work on our Bob videos and inspiration throughout my journey illustrating this book, as well as providing images for pages 32 & 33, & to my son Sebastian for composing awesome music for our videos. I love you both so much!

My Parental Units Glenn & Glenda Brauer, Grandpa & Grandma Richard & Marie Brauer, Brother & Sister-In-Law Richard & Nancye Brauer & our lil' nephew Riley, & my Uncle John Brauer for loving me unconditionally. My life would be empty without you

My "married" family, the entire Martin clan- thanks for accepting me as one of your own. I love all of you :)

Iain Watson & Erin Kalvaitis for being two of my best friends for the past 30 years, Crash LaResh for bringing me along on this adventure with you! And to my "Outdoor Husband" Lurd Tom Odo- You're four of my favoritest weirdos :)

And to all of my other families:
My Living Dead Family, Opera & Stagehand Families, Nest Family, Tent Family (thanks Captain Jim Rose & Ms. BeBe), The Kalvaitis Family, The Hollowell Family, and my new Cat-Astrophe Family

MN
NW

Made in the USA
Charleston, SC
28 April 2016